HERO
Véronique Pittolo
translated by Laura Mullen

BSE

ISBN: 978-0-9997028-0-2

BSE Books are distributed by
Small Press Distribution
1341 Seventh Street
Berkeley, CA 94710
orders@spdbooks.org | www.spdbooks.org | 1-800-869-7553

BSE Books can also be purchased at www.blacksquareeditions.org and www.hyperallergic.com

Contributions to BSE can be made to
Off the Park Press, Inc.
1156 Martine Ave.
Plainfield, NJ 07060
(Please make checks payable to Off the Park Press, Inc.)

To contact the Press please write:
Black Square Editions
1200 Broadway, Suite 3C
New York, NY 10001

An independent subsidiary of Off the Park Press, Inc.
Member of CLMP.

Publisher: John Yau
Editors: Ronna Lebo and Boni Joi
Design & composition: Shanna Compton

Cover art: *Lovers* (1963) by Rosalyn Drexler, acrylic and paper collage on canvas, 55 ¼ x 52 inches. Courtesy of Garth Greenan Gallery, New York, New York. Background photo texture: Rene Böhmer, via Unsplash.

Attempted definition

*The Hero distinguishes himself through his exploits and
a remarkable courage.*

*Legendary and mythic, he demonstrates his valor
through a series of actions and difficult tests.*

*Devoted to a cause, he will be worthy of the public esteem
and glory he has won. Demigod, he must imagine
something heavenly: solar, energetic and resplendent, he faces
the unknown and is never afraid.*

*The Hero is preferably living, but dead, he will be
more effective. The common man, the faithful,
can then identify with him and participate
imaginatively in his existence.*

*Modern Heroes are known through the medium
of audiovisual transmissions (radio, television,
movies). Their superhumanity is visible on the
screen (face enlarged) and audible thanks to an
electronically filtered voice.*

*Actor, cosmonaut, athletic or revolutionary,
young, handsome, rich and amorous, he often
belongs to the universe of the spectacle.*

*The movies engendered these stars who became
idolized heroes, objects of a public cult.*

BILL stops himself brusquely
He enters, stumbles over something.

MURIEL's shoes make two marks on the ground,
two arms dangle from the bed.
He catches his feet in the telephone cord.
He turns around, shuts off the radio.

(Sound of steps amplified on the stairs.)

At this instant the Hero must make a decision,
seize a last chance and prove his autonomy.
The Hero is the guy who's determined to find chances.

The heroine wears a dark raincoat and sunglasses.

A man arrives.
He rests his hand on the barstool beside her.
The conversation starts up, it's 3 in the afternoon.
MURIEL lets things go, the world develops around her, despite her.
Always she leaves traces on the cigarette filters.
Messages, bottles in the sea.

The heroine is a body in movement before being a thought in action.

From the jukebox comes a sweet melody.

> — Jeff? . . .
>
> — . . .
>
> — I'll pass by the drugstore.
> I wanted to tell you how much I think of you.

The man who put his hand on the barstool was spying on her.
BILL knew he was an adversary or perhaps a prospective corpse.
Removing his jacket, he rolls up his sleeves, orders a martini
and brushes off fear like something embarrassing caught on
his clothes.
On the bar, sunglasses signal the presence of MURIEL, sign of
sensual delight.
She leaves, heads toward the convertible, crosses the parking lot.
(The cafeteria was shut.)

The sound of brakes always brings tears to the eyes of the hero.

She fixes her makeup in the rearview mirror.
(The form of the eyes is enough to express the complexity of the face.)

Think of flowers.
It is crucial to arrange as many as possible in the provisional
spaces.

First episode: the lovers' voyage.
Around the Hero, despite him, a history of love is
possible like the air or the hardness of the ground.

His body expresses something.
Close up, you guess his capacity for understanding,
in the movies his end is spectacular.
He swims, battles adversaries, searches the horizon,
incomplete, a projection of his director.
From Madrid to New York, from London to Paris, we meet him
under a variety of appearances with exceptional women.
In the arms of a heroine, we think him gullible.
His approach and his silence have been the object of futile
commentary.
(Like his innocence and his propensity to failure.)
The Hero should not give the certainty of a conclusion
but only fill dead time.

— JEFF,
The speech is cut off.
— You're difficult . . .

In evening clothes in front of a mirror, knotting his tie.

Someone rings. He turns and leaves the visual field.

What does an intense look mean?
How to defend the clumsy gestures?

JEFF doesn't search for words, we recognize him in a significant
detail, his way of appearing or taking on a detached air.
He's always waiting for someone or something,
an event, a recommendation, he follows, is followed,
rarely looks behind him.
We see him pass in front of luxury stores.
Furthermore, he won't age.

(A Hero doesn't age or the actor is exchanged.)

World separated into islands of differentiation.
Each one can see the reality with their eyes, the same
gestures, identical towns and roads without borders.
Limitless world in the precarious conversations.

— Too late, MURIEL . . .

Darkness prevents recognition of the faces' tension.

As he picks up the phone, he takes on a worried air.
We follow the curve of the left eyebrow just to the cheek,
to the collar of his shirt, the excellent quality of the cloth.

— What do you want?

No answer, then we hear the clinking of glasses.
He hangs up.

(In New York, JEFF lives in shirtsleeves, in Paris, a grey or black
suit. People have seen him in London in a green jacket.)

Hanging up, he looks at the bay without saying a word.
BILL knocks at the door.
BILL spends his time waiting for instructions.
Panicked, he'll arrive late at crime scenes.

JEFF tries to make a career in New York,
he returns to New Orleans where he finds the guy who caused
the death of his ex-wife.

The rhythm speeds up:
arrested in the middle of the night, accused of spying.

Time is a notion which goes through the Hero,
time accidentally reckoned, time of cities and airports.

On the airplane, MURIEL recognized in JEFF the daredevil she
used to love.
(The characters leave the descriptive map to enter memory's domain.)
The lover aged . . . Saw him in Atlanta ten years earlier, etc.

*Desire is incomplete, fortuitous, an old or new test, reported. The days
get mixed up, favoring memories of meetings in a lost space, a flat
time, smooth as the surface of a lake.*

Suddenly the heroine returns.
(The airplane lands hard.)

The heroine is necessary to the Hero's validity.
Without her these stories would be limited to a settling of accounts.

Dappled face which prepares itself and strikes the pose,
creature inventing its destiny.
The image assembles itself . . .
We can photograph it mentally:
Heroine just about to . . . at the edge of a catastrophe,
in a spot, a station platform.

MURIEL is known by the sound of her footsteps at night when
she returns and crosses a graveled path.
One hears her walking up to the next story.

Dead, she will be identified at the edge of a lake.
Necessary and supplementary, obvious and unforeseen,
her appearance fades with time but
action remains the sole resource of the feminine partner.

Rain pours down. MURIEL slips into her trench coat.

Most photos are from the time when she was a brunette.
In a square, leaning on a bridge, on her bed leafing through a
magazine or behind the curtains in a hotel corridor.
She leaves lipstick prints on cigarette butts and hairs under pillows.
MURIEL's house is next to a parking lot,
set back from a cafeteria.
Behind: an immense forest, a lake with all sorts
of sounds and stones.
Menacing and reassuring, her room is a fiction.
Bedspread of satin, oval dressing table with multicolored lights.

*Every heroine fixes up the space for her own destiny and tries
to resist betrayal.*

Heroines shift a subtle wind around their silhouette.
Tall and dark, they keep a secret
and their eyes glitter behind their sunglasses.

MURIEL smokes after each meal and turns on the radio
at any hour. She lets the water from her bath overflow.
Truth hidden under makeup.
The light doesn't only come from her face,
and around her nails she can have cut skin with a tendency
to flake.
Encumbered by her body, MURIEL shifts objects without
consequence.

Everyone can imagine her, nude, under her dark hair.

Blonds are less fragile, equally beautiful, with a clear gaze. And in certain sequences, mixed up in a banal intrigue (train, murder, suspicious passengers).

Blond, MURIEL meets JEFF in a bar.

Divided, the Hero defers his declaration.
She observes the way he . . . his body . . . how he lights his cigarettes.
But the Heroine has to wait, the image will become clearer as the emblem of a future love and all its complications.
In the consciousness of heroes, chivalry is not a fundamental stake.

By mistake JEFF's hand touches MURIEL's arm.
In the shadow, the scene passes unperceived.

Patient and passionate, the heroine sees the world transform itself under her eyes:
the body of J., his nonchalance, and the suppleness of his delivery.

(In the past, lovers expressed themselves only by gestures.)

After the shoot, JEFF confesses to his partner that he is not yet
in love. He sees her again the next day under the same lights.
The declaration produces night with its double talk.
Roughness in the voice of a man before a big glass window
darkened by the sky.
Glasses clink.
Strange noises.

The man has his hands on the neck of the woman.

> — He has knotted his tie inside out before
> shutting the door again.

One day, MURIEL was frightened by a displaced chair.
It rained, it was midnight, someone knocked on the door.
The visitor sat near the liquor cabinet.

(Generally, assassins don't leave their card.)

The Hero opens doors,
shuts them soundlessly,
expressing a scarcely formulated hope.

At the fixed hour MURIEL hears the noise of a slammed door.
She is confronted with the problem of resemblance and déjà vu.
She knew this man dressed as a soldier, leading the battle against
his own image.
Then he disappeared from her circle of influence.

Body plastered against the earth, holding his breath,
frequenting infamous places.

Having attained perfection, he no longer evolves.
It's a s if one looked at a landscape from which nothing is missing

This man seeking peace finds the dust of the roads.

Surprised on waking, he reflects and contemplates his white teeth.
Lighting a cigarette, he goes straight to the telephone.

The moment winds up and comes past again:
a man with a pleasant physique leaves his room.
Immediately reminded of about ten different tasks.

(What consistency has the air that he breathes?)

— I'm on hold . . .

Believing he's found a mooring post, here he is with a guitar in place
of a telephone, motionless, on the verge of the ridiculous.
He saves something or someone, an idea, a possible love. The heart's
influence is essential for heroes are made of a pure metal.

Chronologically, the scene of the kiss follows from the solitude of battles
as the result of a certain magic.
(It's that instant when the spectators hold their breath, and totally
identify.)

He rarely expresses himself.
   "The time I spent on television, in the
   demonstrations on the streets, within and without,
   integrated in the world. Things existed before and
   after me, like warning lights.
   Filmed, I didn't feel time passing, but the foam
   produced by the passage from day to night."

JEFF, at the police station:
   "A murder. A woman in the lake.
   BILL threw a stone and the corpse
   came back up."

*A murder is preceded by a tension. The reactions of the assassin come
from an unexpected event like something which upends a previous
reality, for example.*
   "arms grazing the surface of the water"

BILL, against the balustrade:
   "MURIEL!
   It's MURIEL!"**
In the distance a dense curtain of trees.
   — Listen . . .

A shot.

Discouraged, JEFF bypasses the sheriff's office and goes back to
the Packard.

When they come into contact with their partner,
remarkable men make a decision which will have immediate
consequences.
Business is followed by moments of calm, auspicious
for chivalry.

JEFF and MURIEL know from the start that happiness is a
simple and instinctive motion.
The Hero is free when he loves, free from shame as one is free when
one makes one's way through a park.

Regrets exist in order to give a painful consistency to the maturity
of a character.

After several months of happiness, they begin to regret their adventure.
At first they enjoyed a reciprocity without constraint, "man-with-cigarettes" and "woman in the red dress."
An attraction without effort like beginning a conversation.

The work of the eyes was done.

At the heart of the dialogue, faces take on a sharper outline.
Answers come before the questions
which are punctuated by furtive gestures.
Little by little the world adjusts to this situation.

The woman crosses her legs and reflects under her long false lashes.

The provisional character of the moment is shattered by the ringing telephone.

In love stories the telephone plays a part as a guarantee of continuity.
Someone cuts off a speech, Someone fills in the silences.
The breathing of MURIEL: sustained palpitations.
The sighs of JEFF: a calm puff.
The man sets down his lighter, engraved with initials.

They find themselves in a seaside resort although
MURIEL prefers freshwater resorts.
The hotel is a crescent built to follow the curve of the bay.
There's the wind, trees, promenaders walking slowly. Sails,
windowpanes, reflections of the shadowed plaza.

The rendezvous has a provisional value.
The man waits for the woman or vice versa.
Each one makes an effort to arrive last.

Sea calm as a lake.

MURIEL replaced the handset, emotion intact.
JEFF wears a new shirt.
He looks at himself in the glass, changes his expression, his
cigarette burns down to a precarious ash.

First meeting like the first time one sees the ocean, together or
separately.
Profiles exposed, the heroes paced the town for hours.

The day before, they were not in the story,
not yet in this eventful world
with the necessary density to receive them.

First exit as one goes out in the evening, accompanied,
to the edge of the water, by the sadness which consists in
deciphering an expression.

We understand: two protagonists and soon a kiss.
We not aware of their end and the importance of confessions.
The nails of the woman reflect objects like tiny mirrors.

In a second, JEFF forgets the crucial words.

*The characters leave the frame as if extracted from a book or a film,
like flowers planted in a park, useless but communicating the fragility
of appearances.*

They present themselves:
Blond in suit or brunette in low-cut red.
The man with his simple, methodical gestures.
*By definition, heroes are masculine, because women have fewer models
than men.*
They recognize each other by the level of their solitude.
*Once the mission's accomplished, they age and one perceives a weakness
in their way of walking.*

Tomorrow, in an hour, a passion begins.

Deserted jetty.
Everything's there: the waves, the roofs and the blue, the black-eyed heroine sitting in front of an opaque glass.
Eyes hidden by huge sunglasses.
On her features, a fleeting worry, a groundless doubt.

"At the edge of the water" means we shift the frame to the limits of description.
We wait for something without foreseeing the monotony of the landscape associated with the encounter.
Our characters use the space to the fullest:
road, sky, body crossed by reflexes.
The void threatens, absence of retorts.

JEFF chooses his thoughts, calls the bartender and orders a "double of something" which resonates in the tepid air.

(Heroes are often submitted to a sonorous space which entirely contains them.)
The water solidifies.
Then the sea is mixed up with a lake and a deserted parking lot.

What was Mr. H. thinking of at the wheel of his convertible?

According to a logical process, his driving is enough to give a global vision of the world.
We know he believes in the innocence of MURIEL, heroine placed at the heart of a complicated romance.

Honks the horn.
Brakes in the pedestrian crossing.

Back hunched, eyes sharp for potential prey.

At the wheel, heroes don't think, they content themselves with representing their category.
Neither the quickness nor the gleam of the hood are enough for the elegance of the character, his deceptive power.
The automobile forms a kind of charming atmosphere, like a tuxedo.

In record time, JEFF avoids the accident, making his tires squeal.
At the edge of the action, in the suspended effort,
he circles the traps destiny sets for him, passes and scatters,
mobile face toward the danger.

"Let's not be too hard on fear,
sometimes fear makes things better."

At 3 p.m. exactly, MURIEL glances in the rearview mirror.
Someone's following her.
She takes a left in front of the station, then circles the docks.

3:45, the man's still there.
From the docks a layer of smoke lifts, mixes with the sadness of
a day's end.

In silence a red convertible leaves the parking lot.
MURIEL orders a bluish alcohol with a lot of ice.

Unique and essential method of transportation with air-conditioning
and electric cigar holder.
For the Hero, every trajectory is punctuated by stations and
inscriptions.

Wind in his hair, JEFF settles himself on the leather seat.
Reserved, blasé, solitary.
Smooth drive on a deserted road.
Envied, coveted, such is Mr H. in the eyes of the pedestrians.
Foot on the gas: motion of trees and vibrant light.

Blinded, JEFF knows we look at him.
He himself sketches the line of the horizon as a function of
his speed.
Curves, road signs, reflections on the face of his watch.
Shirtsleeves rolled up to the elbow.
A puff of wind, then the road's clear again.

Generally, heroes are not conscious of their freedom.

At the movies, characters come and go, accumulating promises.
Their truth is a red warning sign, a light which lasts after the word
END, *in the melancholy streets. The distance amplifies the seduction,*
we see again the face of the actress before her disappearance.

Faces are problematic ideas:
MURIEL gives herself the features of another, disguises her
nature with a coarse elegance.
Under her makeup, we see the boredom with everything, the
isolation, the silence.

Carnal, the heroine accumulates false graces and useless proposals, loses
herself in a forced smile.
In a novel, she hesitates between a language of reason and the words
dictated by the heart.

The face of MURIEL could have been as mysterious as her body.

Russian model:

> — A day at home? What tedium!
> Remove your gloves, give orders to a minor
> official:
> — You're not going to the committee meeting?
> It's all the same to me, I promised ANNA
> KARENINA I'd swing by to pick her up.

Action:

Two enemies in conflict separated by a street. A leaf falls.
The shot reverberates although the scene has no witness.
What's at stake in the drama: a woman, a sum of money, a secret.

*The heroine will love the winner, especially if he dies before her, but
one does not make an actor die for 1 million dollars.*

"Why kill Heroes?"

The Hero has no family, only limited connections with the world.
Gloomy or in color, he submits to a photogenic experience.

There's always someone who photographed him at different periods of
his life: filming, at the wheel, at the negotiating table.
Relaxed in front of an audience.
Portraits and pieces of evidence, documents in which time has gouged
some wrinkles.

Hero of evening and morning, crossing the squares and cutting
through crowds, sitting, standing, walking in the tumult, approaching
women with a flattering speech.

Photos of the Hero are published in the major newspapers and
illustrated magazines.

JEFF was to meet MURIEL in the diner,
BILL shows up in his place.
MURIEL throws herself into his arms because she dreamed he
saved her life.

The sky takes on multiple hues soon enough.
The customers efface themselves.
We hear each character breathe.
(JEFF had always accepted everything about MURIEL.)

The conversation rises a notch in the bar that will be deserted.
Suddenly a victim arrives and begins to play her role.
She takes the stool, jostles the Hero.
A huge silence precedes what follows.

An argument sputters out and the victim is accidentally killed.

In theory, killers are famous after they've left their town.

Every nocturnal thriller is both a story of love and of disappearance.

Struck matches, brakes and the noise of the motor.

The assassin runs alongside a facade at the edge of the canal
where barges pass loaded with coal.
Without losing his cool, he puts the corpse in the trunk of his car.
Wrapped in a sheet and tied up, the dead person is a mysterious
package.

> — On the gleaming tiles, the blood forms a well-
> defined dark puddle.

At first the victim doesn't realize someone's talking to her.
(Victims are affable and naive.)

> — The statuette . . . on the mantelpiece!

She scarcely sees her executioner as she collapses with the sound
of a corpse on the waxed parquet.
The record's still turning when J. leaves the room.

Two theories clash: several killers and two categories of victim, the willing and the cursed.
Victims are usually in need, they never think ahead.
There's also the nonchalant creature who forgets the keys inside her house.
Those surprised by the continuous blare of a horn.
How to return what they are owed?

Every Monday, MURIEL walks to her hairdresser's.
She wears woven open-toed pumps.
Nail polish scaled and formed vertical lines like red lipstick at the corners of the lips.
First stage, we expect her silhouette to open the gate.

Long hair, between 25 and 30 years old.
Street to the left.

> *"When shadowing, one must always pay attention to the details."*

The future victim takes shortcuts.
Around her, cars brake and accelerate continuously.

Rule #1: never cross their gaze.

To fill space and stay in motion while using shop windows and the rearview mirror.
To stop in a blind spot, to adopt the behavior of the person followed.

Summer evening, everything's sticky.
Yellow reflections in the motionless lake.
It was chosen for the scene of the drama because of the large trees lining the bank.
Because of the absence of witnesses.
Fir trees and flowers embalming.
A heady perfume attracts the heroine to the edge of the danger.
The mystery woman is ready for the beautiful depth of the water.
In the distance, a small boat tilts and rights itself.

MURIEL leans over, the handrail snaps, the bridge, last connections to the perceptible world.

We recover a patent leather court shoe from the bottom of the boat.

Since the accident we had taken for a murder, since the drama,
the heroes bore themselves.
They pass long hours in fashionable places, raising half-empty
glasses of champagne.
— Mister?

When they come in everyone stops talking:

Going into the lounge, Mr H. found himself at the center of the
conversations, he played well, we identified with him in this role,
he was happy and hadn't dreamed of his fame.

MURIEL flops onto the sofa.
The mirror makes her hair shine.
She whispered while drawing on her cigarette.

(Much later the Hero becomes her lover.)

Love scenes are filmed according to the real desire of the actors, who know that in life, as at the movies, appointments are a prelude to seduction.

Each one adjusts their gaze to the other.
If we give the Hero exclusive rights to the role of lover, the story will circle back on itself after a few declarations.

It doesn't matter where passion is born, on a journey, a bridge, a night passed in a dimly-lit bar.
Among a range of subtle possibilities.
For a relatively long time, the two characters remain calm and silent. Hands linked and useless.

(The heroes who reach their happiness are patient.)

The hazards of existence meant they were used to timed meetings.
They separate after an hour and a half of talking for reasons which have nothing to do with emotion.

JEFF becomes a pilot and rediscovers MURIEL as an airline stewardess.

Flushing out the heroine is a delicate operation:
we surprise the natural falseness of a laugh and the movement of a
neck, a more pronounced dimple on the left.
The world should enter the character and not the reverse.

We imagine BILL has always been nervous in front of lakes and expanses of trees.
He is chosen to identify the victim while MURIEL and JEFF, in the studio next door, rehearse a scene of reunion.

BILL has an office in an important agency where he handles
delicate business.
He eats at a set time.

One day, some men waited for him.
The meeting was short, the shot rang out, covered by the passing
of a truck.

The memory of the mediocre Hero fails after he's wounded.
He mops his brow and looks at the sheriff with eyes full of hope.

> — What do you want?
> — . . . to help you . . .

Before arriving at the lake, BILL had a premonition,
the fear of dying before the last red fire.

> — If I die . . . my code name is **Verity Chase**.
> 10 million dollars and you'll never see me again.

After a hectic sequence, the characters again become anonymous individuals.

Secrecy suits the back side of the scenery.

Someone moves along the lifeless corridors, half opening doors. The dressing room of the actress is a space cluttered with false declarations and mascara.

The heroine no longer hides herself beneath glowing makeup, she can do without expression.
No longer that woman who moves according to an artificial process.
After each shoot she changes her activity,
goes incognito at the beach resorts and becomes again this brunette who resembles everyone.

She dines alone "Chez Tom" at a table at the back.

The solitary Hero is never tired.

In a group, the heroic dimension tends to disappear,
one melts into an undifferentiated mass.
Danger will be needed to restart the action.

JEFF is kidnapped at 11:45 in a limousine.
Yesterday, he wore a red shirt.

After the abduction, his destiny swerves.
Then the action depends on deceived hope, it no longer meets
our expectations.
Actors and spectators are taken hostage in a precise dramatic
development. If he can get out, the reprieved Hero improves his
reputation.
If he's murdered, we will remember his casualness.

Where do the strongest moments go?

"When I returned to the house,
I dreamed I was the Hero of that magnetic gaze."

In voice and gesture, a feeling passes lightly.

Let's take JEFF's shoes:
The shoes of the Hero are black and shiny.
They reveal a slow or fast pace,
the fact of coming and going and making doors creak.
Shoes lengthen the body according to the pleat of the trousers.

In order to travel, JEFF will need well-made shoes which suit a supple elegance.

However, the Hero remains in an unresolved conflict,
a consciousness which he ignores.

> "No one knows my true nature.
> I climb to my room with dignity."

*The first time he heard his name on the radio, JEFF became a
character, a fiction.*

*In a rolled collar, from the back or in profile in a luxury hotel.
If no one sees him, he doesn't change.*

*Rooms empty themselves, waiting rooms.
As soon as he isn't appealed to, solitude isolates him a little more.
We don't know what he's looking at, but his view sweeps the tall
silver buildings.
The city where he'll hide himself in case of failure is constructed with
reflections and sharp angles.*

*Compact, fortified, such is the city of the modern Hero, brilliant
and spacious.*

Most of the time, JEFF is on a mission, in a magical light which
itemizes his features in detail.
At night, his silhouette slows down, one notices the pale collar
which differentiates him from the crowd.

> — No one knows me.
> I'm the invisible man.

Is he immortal?

He needs movement and leaves a profound nostalgia in his wake.

MURIEL compares him to an unknown perfume.
She thinks of him while smoking long blue cigarettes, ignoring the future.
From the terrace she sees the hills and dreams she becomes
MELINDA, SUZY, or GLENDA.
A pearl choker gleams on her neck,
focal point of her character.
(The autopsy will reveal evidence of strangulation.)
Moreover she dreams her life is in danger,
she's hunted by strange individuals.
She will age 20 years in 10 minutes.

(According to BILL, a suicide would have left her jewels on the embankment.)

Heroic names call up qualities which refer to precise situations:
JEFF designating the lover and adventurer,
We make BILL an anxious individual.

MURIEL corresponds to that ephemeral instant in which a body
disappears.

One would say:

> "The woman was wearing a choker and had
> shoulder-length hair."

Or:

> "A feminine voice made itself heard."

Or again:

> "She telephoned J. who gave
> the message to B."

It's important that the Hero knows to alter his name according to the
state of his soul.

JEFF goes toward the telephone.
Without altering his posture he brings the handset to his ear.
Then he walks automatically into a room.
He comes back down in a new suit.

This time the rendezvous takes place at the edge of a pool.
Noon in front of the turquoise rectangle.

MURIEL is physically affected by the presence of her partner,
whom she indifferently names JACK or JEFF, BILL or JOHN.
Endowed with a devastating beauty taut at the edges of her face,
she exposes herself and takes risks.
Pouring her a drink, JEFF avoids her eyes.

Synchronized with the dialogue the anxiety mounts.

The heroine curls her upper lip and turns her head.
Her bikini forms an accidental stain in the composition of the
whole.

— The documents?

The man remained cold.
The glasses sparkling in the heat.
The next appointment was booked for 4 p.m..

Generally, the heroine finds her autonomy in tragic scenes:
MURIEL while fighting, ANNA KARENINA under the train, or
again the anonymous creature we see crossing deserted parking lots.

In bars, airports, on bridges, morning or night, alone, accompanied,
blond or brunette, hunted, stupid and mortal.
For some life becomes a battle, for others a series of appointments and
nights out.

They exist in order to indicate an imminent danger.
The flowers, the train, the pool are reference points.
The water is always opaque and the blossoms too fragrant.

MURIEL waits for the signal which will transform her into a
creature.
She spends her time seeking out emotion.

(If her partner was only an empty envelope?
A face wrapped in bandages and dark glasses?)

"I walk," says JEFF,
"I'm living, the blood flows in my veins.
There's the water, a stretch with trees."

The heroine's on the bridge, flags flutter in a logical way.
Thin dress, nothing is definite, not the sky nor the benches
lining the space.
Our characters come forward to the edge of the scenery,
soon they will belong to a time that's gone.

*Sometimes one waits for a feeling but it doesn't happen, then it's
necessary to compromise, to deliver the standard phrase.*

Faced by danger, the Hero has few alternatives.

The image shatters.
Finally, feeling intervenes.

What really happens in the vicinity of the Hero?
In the big turmoil of air which shakes his consciousness.
And in the landscape where he evolved?

How to interpret the hesitation which consists in taking one way
for another?

In moments of great willpower, his pupils resemble a dark crystal.

It's understood that JEFF walked with fluid ease in a scene almost
real, thanks to him we recover the closeness of things.
Basic sensations and a place to go.

We finally itemized some actions.

His time divides into minutes more or less vast.
The nights are fuller, more tender than the days, for darkness develops
passions, the ideal moment for inventing a fatal conception of
existence.

Night of the hero, colorless and nameless,
undifferentiated mass.
Against the blackness the cinema marquees glow:

"MURIEL: A ROMANCE."

At 8 years old, she wanted to be an actress:
for JEFF, a film,
for BILL, a lighter style.
She wished for cruises where one travels incognito, nocturnal
ventures where headlights shine on the lunar crescent of a bay.
Silence, the awkwardness when the ignition's switched off.
Keys sparkle with a singular brightness, gazes meet.

How to give desire a third dimension?

Desires are like faces, never fixed.

Features vary according to the light, the voice and countenance change
according to circumstances, the nose is usually perfect.
Fragile balance between forehead and mouth.

In photographs, the skin seems clearer.
Soon enough we understand the role of appearances.

One hand on the wheel, JEFF takes on a determined air.
The baton lifts.

(Collapse of the Hero.)

He staggers back up, rubbing his forehead.

The woman intervenes as a guarantee of balance:
at her touch, the Hero acquires some humanity.

JEFF needs MURIEL's desire and sometimes the appearance of BILL.
His reactions are controlled like scheduled flights from an airport.

After having vanquished the enemy, he recalls his exploits before
a turbulent gathering.
The sun goes down behind the blinds.
Our man is tall and relaxed.
Then we imagine his reactions when faced with a forced
departure, a tragic alternative.
His profile alone determines the set of the body, lightly shifted
toward the horizon.

Already we hear birds skim the hillside in search of their prey.
The drama is preceded by a profound silence invested in the
throats of the spectators.

After the shot, someone asks if the enemies arrived before dawn.
The discussion gets lively then silence again swoops down on the
assembly,

> "silence of the open country before the departure of
> the herd."

Every duel indicates a tension between two opponents.
The weaker Hero is going to die.
There should be vice, remorse,
the heroine is going to throw herself into the arms of the winner.

Next MURIEL says she followed him all the way to his hotel,
the sun glowed in BILL's pupils.
She knows the difference between "the expression of the gaze" and
"the color of the eyes" and that heroes generally have pale eyes.

At this time they're leading a nocturnal existence, developing a
relative hostility around their presence.

One day a car behind them will accelerate, tires hissing in the rain.

A hand at the edge of a sleeve:

— The revolver!

MURIEL, blond, turns around.
Change in the hairdo and an effort to assess the speed of the movement.

Heroes really live the image they return to us as a precise memory (bedroom, deserted road, bus station).
Each detail works to develop the effects of surprise and expectation.

Shards of an embrace:

— Never to see you again!

Voluptuous pleasure cancels every attempt at compromise.

In the middle of the kiss, JEFF continues to reflect on his fate.
In love, incidental situations stimulate him:
turmoil, the impossibility of expressing himself, awkwardness
considered as determining episode.
Several times he suggests to the heroine a way to reach
happiness.
In vain.

She responds with mixed feelings,
Preoccupied by a flight reflex.

— I leave tomorrow on a mission, etc.

*In one such tension, it's the turn of the Hero to express what we hope
(despair transformed into joy).*
*Thus heroism is bound to a reversal which is fulfilled in the change of
heart, the link, the reunions.*

*But if love triumphs, it gives way to a shared restlessness as we don't
know the real feelings that drive each character.*

In life as in fiction, one makes appointments. One arrives early and the other finds an excuse.

Theoretically, we fall in love at the same time.
Nothing extraordinary, passion born of a spontaneous momentum.
We recognize ourselves in the ordeal of noise, chaos, the crowd.
The process of identification prompts future lovers to prolong a respectful silence.

Isolated, the Hero arouses a profound nostalgia.

If we consider MURIEL from behind at the end of a film, we will experience something like a catastrophe, an absurd regret.
On the contrary, if she meets up again with the main actor, we will have a feeling of being split and overflowing.

First scenario:
Heart pounding, he opens the door.
A perfume spills immediately.
The heroine turns around coughing and one sees the nape of
her neck.
Lashes in relief, a choker.
Sound of breathing.
At the third sigh, the pearls fall one by one.

A telephone rings, we hear heels.
Creaking door, thin line of blue light.
Voice.

Second ring. Sound of slammed doors.
Vanishing cry.
While embracing, the partners think of something else.
Too great a concentration might make the characters ridiculous.

Another possibility:
They get back to New Orleans by steep roads.
JEFF keeps the handkerchief found in the victim's pocket.

Before getting lucky, heroes look for evidence and find clues.
Evidence of the encounter, that the corpse has been discovered, that it's
a question of a lake and not a beach.

Signs of recognition:
playboys and pinups in the convertible.
Turns at 90 miles per hour. Deserted highways.
Reflections of tall buildings in warm pupils.
Excited gestures.
Spotless hands and leather shoes which make no sound when fear
catches up.

Proof that the actions have been itemized hour by hour, that JEFF
buys his outfits in the big luxury stores, and MURIEL passes the
time in bathrooms.

The abduction of the hero has obscure ramifications.
This event quickens the mystery of otherness.

> *— Did he organize the thing with the help of an accomplice?*
> *—Where are the documents?*
> *—Whose side is his partner on?*

The hunted hero belongs to a category which discovers subterfuges by
leaving town.
He's given a false code number and his telephone rings in the void.
He'll pretend to return drunk, a corpse on his shoulders.
If he's kidnapped the fiancée of a rival Hero,
he will have killed that one with a knife.

After years of silence, we rediscover him running a shabby restaurant.
From a distance, his silhouette deceives but the closer he gets, the more
the Hero exists.

Through a melancholy way of declaring himself.

Years are necessary to discover the person behind the performance.
Fear, like the rest, the Hero tests without controlling.
In the center of town or on the highway, by accident. The suspicion
lasts a minute, then existence takes a sudden turn toward something
brutal.

A flash of glass hurls JEFF out of the vehicle.
He rolls in the dust and loses his austere elegance.
Lifeless body, flattened, inert in a blackish puddle.

The heroine intervenes crying.

The lovers struggle between a minute of silence and the nostalgic end.

An accident can also have the sweetness of recaptured love.

A parked taxi.
JEFF paid in dollars.
The bar was dimly lit.
Long hall with an orchestra at the end.

MURIEL dances with someone unknown.
The music stops.
The man tries to kiss her.

The Hero intervenes after the second song.

It's after having freed the heroine that JEFF suggests a cigarette.

In two hours we will know all:
Soft legs and fresh face, undulating hips,
a suit for day, at night, a red dress with a zipper.
MURIEL will be at the center of some worries and interests.

The next day, one offers her flowers, a watch and a glossy purse.
We will recognize her by the jangle of the keys to her convertible.

JEFF will come by each night to take her out.
Time without danger, time of the little pointy heels.
Cushions of silk and nocturnal dances.
Then the returns, the delays, the feverish wait.
He calls from towns whose names escape him.

Before each meeting, a cognac.
The sun crosses the windowpanes of the salon, lights up the
frames, the walls where the photos of Mr. H. are hung.
MURIEL sometimes finds it difficult to identify him in his true
form. She finds him too large in the photographs.

*Images are no longer enough to authenticate the personality of
the Hero.*
*City by city, he fashions his destiny and receives many letters
beginning:*

> "My favorite star,
> Dear idol, I've seen you 5 times in
> *Tell Me Why?*"

*We collect photographs, press cuttings, declarations which evoke a love
brought to term.*
*We remember the terrace, the trees, and the bench where he spoke to his
partner for the first time.*

> "The man took the woman very
> seriously but she stepped away from the bridge
> to go toward the car"

This time, the woman takes the initiative and waits to kiss her Hero.

Eyes fluttering, she clutches her purse tight against a yellow-
beige suit.

For a long time one believed that heroes were confined to a frame.

Frame of life, television screen, window open or shut.
How do their feet touch the ground?
A sound of footsteps drags them from solitude, and immediately time accumulates on the surface of their features.
Beginning then the impossible missions and dangerous journeys, the coded conversations.
Stopped trains, glistening footbridges and streets.

The movement of MURIEL is pinpointed by the echo of her heels on the pavement.

We recall the time she waited for JEFF on the deck of a boat, and also when she descended from the train with her little black purse.

The time when JEFF held the door for her, extremely gallant.
When his body was enveloped in an inaccessible substance.
When his gestures were scarcely tense.

Leaving the car, the characters have that light movement of the
shoulders which characterizes heroes, that mute elegance.
Far from the world, the fatal sequence unfolds near an area lined with
black trees.
The sky becomes entirely red, shadows take their places.

The victim doesn't fall yet.

The world trembles, one hears the noise of a motor.
The instant is a suspended screech of brakes.
She still doesn't fall.
First shadow which moves.
Dry sound of a gate.

The trees begin to vibrate, everything solid dissolves.
In one second the features of MURIEL transform themselves.
She loses her footing, loses herself, heads toward failure.

When death is swift, one doesn't have time to review one's entire life.

In exposing themselves the heroes give up their truth and secrete oblivion.

One day their blood hardens, the skull becomes a cracked mirror, no longer managing the paradoxical idea of permanence and movement.

Heroism is an incomplete notion.
BILL lacks the qualities to become JEFF.
MURIEL would have needed reflection and judgment, but each victim acts according to the ferocity of their environment.

As an old man, JEFF rediscovers her silhouette while watching television.
MURIEL appears at the end of the film.
Long legs and an hour-glass figure, the winning smile, same as before.

Sometimes the heroines distance themselves, backs straight and heads held high.
Brunettes have an alarming efficiency.

THE END

Acknowledgments

Selections from the translation have appeared in *Chicago Post-Modernism* and the *Oomph* anthology. Laura Mullen wishes to thank those editors, and then Cole Swensen and Hanna Roberts-Williams for the guidance and insights, as well as Louisiana State University (the sabbatical), and the Trelex Residency in Paris (where this translation was completed), as well as John Yau and Shanna Compton at Black Square, and then, last but most, Véronique Pittolo, for her patience and faith.

About the Author

Véronique Pittolo was born in Douai, France, and now lives in Paris. She is the author of over fifteen books and several multimedia works and she has won prizes for her work, including the 2004 SGDL (Société des Gens de Lettres) award and Yvan Goll prize. She teaches writing in a variety of venues in Paris including the Institut Gustave Roussy.

About the Translator

Laura Mullen is the McElveen Professor in English at LSU and the author of eight books. Her recent works include a collaboration with the artist John David O'Brien: *Verge*.